SIGHT WORDS

PART 2 — O to Z

SECOND BOOK

INCLUDES ACTIVITIES & GAMES

www.aceacademicpublishing.com

Author: Ace Academic Publishing

Ace Academic Publishing is a leading supplemental educational workbook publisher for grades K-12. At Ace Academic Publishing, we realize the importance of imparting analytical and critical thinking skills during the early ages of childhood and hence our books include materials that require multiple levels of analysis and encourage the students to think outside the box.

The materials for our books are written by award winning teachers with several years of teaching experience. All our books are aligned with state standards and are widely used by many schools throughout the country.

Prepaze is a sister company of Ace Academic Publishing. Intrigued by the unending possibilities of the internet and its role in education, Prepaze was created to spread the knowledge and learning across all corners of the world through an online platform. We equip ourselves with state-of-the-art technologies so that knowledge reaches the students through the quickest and the most effective channels.

For enquiries and bulk orders, contact us at the following address:

3736, Fallon Road, #403
Dublin, CA 94568
www.aceacademicpublishing.com

This book contains copyrighted material. The purchase of this material entitles the buyer to use this material for personal and classroom use only. Reproducing the content for commercial use is strictly prohibited. Contact us to learn about options to use it for an entire school district or other commercial use.

ISBN: 978-1-949383-19-5
© Ace Academic Publishing, 2020

PARENT'S GUIDE

Use this book to introduce your child to an exciting new new passion for reading and writing. This book will not only improve your child's communication skills, the colorful puzzles will make learning a fun activity!

Other books from Ace Academic Publishing

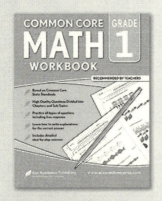 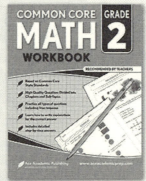 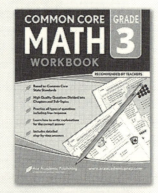 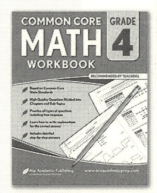
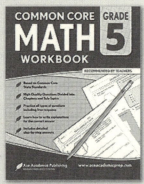 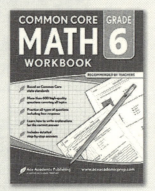 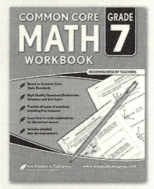 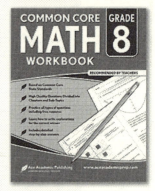

Hello Everyone!

We are happy to learn
sight words with you...
Shall we start?
Let's go!

Beware of the dog!

I am kind of happy.

I am short of money.

Wind blew my house off.

It has cooled off.

The alarm went off.

 I often travel.

We go there often.

 He often helps others.

 This book is old.

I am 6 years old.

 That is an old castle.

 Put your hat on.

The light is on.

 He sat on the bench.

 Only one person was there to witness it.

Choose one person.

 I will buy a new one.

 Are you an only child?

I only slept two hours.

 My house is only a mile away from here.

 It is now or never.

Is that a cat or a dog?

 Hurry, or you will miss the train.

 We love each other.

Do you have any other questions?

 They moved in just the other day.

 That is our project.

He accepted our offer.

 He acted as our guide.

 The team is out of the league.

Put out the light on the stage.

 We ran out of food.

 What is over there in space?

He must be over fifty.

 I am looking over his report.

Try it out!

Fill in the blanks with the words that are provided in the boxes below.

| or | often | off | out | our | other |

It has cooled __off__ .

He acted as __out__ guide.

He _____ helps others.

Is that a cat _____ a dog?

We love each _____ .

We ran _____ of food.

Try it out!

Write your own sentence based on the sight words given below.

| or | often | off | out | our | other |

Let's learn opposites.

 He has his own room.

They have their own satellite.

 Did you do this on your own?

 Do you have a part time job?

I left part of the meal uneaten.

 Tom took part in the summer festival.

PEOPLE

They are good people.

Be kind to old people.

Forty people were present.

PLACE

You are in a safe place.

He went in place of me for the trip.

This place is large.

She has a point.

I do not see your point.

The knife has a sharp point.

Put your coat on.

Who put you up to it?

Put the luggage down.

You are a quite man.

He seems quite happy.

That is quite a story.

I am really tired.

I really like that!

That is really good!

 That is right!

Are you all right?

 Call up Ed right away.

 She said goodbye.

What he said is not true.

 He said, "It is nine o'clock.

 Are they all the same?

I am the same age.

 Give me the same, please.

 Say it clearly.

What did he say?

 Did you say something?

Try it out!

Fill in the blanks with the words that are provided in the boxes below.

| right | put | quite | own | really | same |

Are you all _____ ?

They have their _____ satellite.

_____ the luggage down.

I _____ like that.

Call up Ed _____ away.

You are a _____ man.

Try it out!

Write your own sentence based on the sight words given below.

| right | put | quite | own | really | same |

Challenge yourself to a picture sudoku.

Solution

SCHOOL

 Dad carried me to school.

She goes to school.

 When does school end?

SEE

 See you again.

I see a lion.

 I want to see the movie.

 I would have seen the chopper.

I have seen enough.

 You should have seen her face.

 Tom set a trap.

You should always set a good example.

 The prisoners were set free.

She smiled.

She is happy.

She can skate.

You should sleep.

What should I bring?

You should try to see it.

SIDE

 Lie down on your left side.

He went over to the other side.

 I felt a sudden pain in my side.

SINCE

 We have been friends ever since we were kids.

Steve & Ed have known each other since last year.

 He has been playing tennis since this morning.

 This car is small.

This bag is too small for the book.

 Can you see that small horse?

 I am so happy!

It will not take so long.

 I play golf every so often.

 I need some paper.

We ate some apple.

 This tire needs some air.

 Did you say something?

I want something to eat.

 Please do something about it.

Try it out!

Fill in the blanks with the words that are provided in the boxes below.

| should | so | side | something | small | school |

Lie down on your left _____.

Dad carried me to _____.

You _____ try to see it.

It will not take _____ long.

This car is _____.

I want _____ to eat.

Try it out!

Write your own sentence based on the sight words given below.

| should | so | side | something | small | school |

Crossword

Challenge yourself to a crossword puzzle.

Across

1. We love each _____.
2. He has been playing tennis _____ this morning.
3. I _____ travel.
4. He seems _____ happy.

Down

5. Call up Ed _____ away.
6. Be kind to old _____.
7. She goes to _____.
8. Did you say _____?

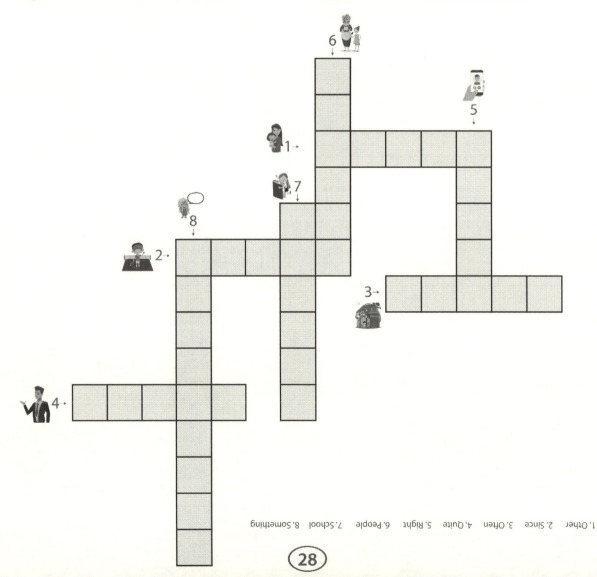

1. Other 2. Since 3. Often 4. Quite 5. Right 6. People 7. School 8. Something

He is still here.

Is the fish still alive?

My legs still hurt.

I have never seen such a large whale.

He is above doing such a thing.

Jack is such a good boy!

TAKE

Take it easy while driving.

Let me take a look.

Take a deep breath.

I am taller than you.

He is stronger than you.

Gold is heavier than silver.

 Is my cooking that good?

That was an excellent shot.

 Not that I have heard of.

 The sun is up.

That is the way.

 Turn on the TV.

Their eyes met.

I have asked for their approval.

They must repair their car.

All of them went there.

The news made them happy.

I invited them to the party.

 We were younger then.

Take a deep breath and then relax.

 I drank milk and then went to bed.

 There is no doubt.

I wanted to go there.

 Is there an elevator?

These dogs are big.

These pearls look real.

These scissors cut well.

They got married.

They gave a star to me.

They are playing chess.

Try it out!

Fill in the blanks with the words that are provided in the boxes below.

| there | than | the | these | take | that |

He is stronger _____ you.

_____ was a excellent shot.

Is _____ an elevator?

_____ a deep breath.

_____ sun is up.

_____ pearls look real.

Try it out!

Write your own sentence based on the sight words given below.

| there | than | the | these | take | that |

Find the object using jumbled letters and fill in the space below.

 I think it is OK!

Please think about it.

 I think it is worth a try.

 This is it.

Can I eat this?

 I love this photo.

 Those are my books.

Whose shoes are those?

 What happened to those DVD's?

 I thought she was sick.

That is what I thought.

 I thought you had to get up by 7:30.

 I have three dogs.

I only spent three dollars.

 I caught three fish yesterday.

 I am through with my work.

We breathe through your nose.

 He was looking through a microscope.

 Talk to me!

Go to sleep.

 Give it to him.

 I told him to come.

She told him a joke.

 Guess what he told me?

 It is too loud.

That is too good.

 Do not add too much salt.

 I took a walk.

He took my hand.

 He took a day off.

 I have two cars.

Two seats were vacant.

 Two ice creams, please!

 The building is under construction.

There is a cat under the tree.

 You are under arrest.

Try it out!

Fill in the blanks with the words that are provided in the boxes below.

| told | think | two | to | those | took |

Whose shoes are _____?

He _____ a day off.

I have _____ cars.

I _____ him to come.

Give it _____ him.

I _____ it is ok!

44

Try it out!

Write your own sentence based on the sight words given below.

| told | think | two | to | those | took |

Let's learn opposites.

| OPAQUE | TRANSPARENT | DIRTY | CLEAN |

| SAD | HAPPY | LIGHT | DARK |

| FULL | EMPTY | CARELESS | CAUTIOUS |

I will stay here until ten.

Wait until further notice.

Until I hear from him.

Wash it up.

Somehow I stood up!

Prices went up.

US

Come with us.

Pass us the cards.

He teaches us Chemistry.

USE

I use a cloth bag.

Could I use your desk?

What will you use it for?

It is very cold.

He takes very good care of his mother.

He is very fast.

I want a guitar.

What do you want?

I do not want dinner.

 I was shot.

I was tired.

 She was brave.

 That is the way.

He is confident in the way he looks.

 He observed the way, the birds flies.

 We are happy.

We enjoy talking.

 We are in a hurry.

 She sings well.

Well, let us go.

 This knife cuts well.

 I went out.

The closet went up.

 I went on reading.

 I wish I were rich.

Were you busy yesterday?

 There were two cakes.

Try it out!

Fill in the blanks with the words that are provided in the boxes below.

| us | well | was | very | those | went |

This knife cuts _____.

The closet _____ up.

He teaches _____ Chemistry.

I _____ shot.

That is the _____.

It is _____ cold!

Try it out!

Write your own sentence based on the sight words given below.

| us | well | was | very | those | went |

WORD PUZZLE

Challenge yourself to a word puzzle and try to find the words:
Than, Them, These, Through, Until, Use, Went and When.

h	t	g	b	p	a	u	s	e	j	i	f	d	c	o	h
n	l	t	t	e	k	m	d	i	r	g	a	b	n	t	c
f	c	h	b	r	j	u	n	t	i	l	o	h	k	h	t
s	a	e	m	d	h	f	c	k	b	t	g	j	d	a	e
t	e	s	l	z	k	j	c	e	t	h	e	m	i	n	f
h	n	e	e	w	h	e	n	o	k	a	m	b	r	j	c
r	j	f	c	s	b	r	f	i	e	d	k	h	u	o	l
o	t	i	w	k	t	h	e	s	e	e	c	b	s	m	z
u	h	d	e	e	b	a	l	g	f	z	k	i	e	j	g
g	e	k	n	j	t	p	c	b	t	h	r	o	u	g	h
h	f	o	t	b	r	k	f	m	c	e	a	h	f	c	j
n	t	h	e	m	e	h	u	e	j	d	s	b	k	l	f
l	c	g	b	f	j	i	n	a	k	w	h	e	n	o	c
p	t	r	a	k	d	e	t	e	j	b	f	t	h	a	n
k	w	e	n	t	j	o	i	n	b	t	e	a	h	b	g
e	b	a	i	g	f	r	l	e	d	l	k	c	p	h	c

55

Solution:

What is that?

What did you buy?

I know what to do.

When do you study?

When was it finished?

Do it when you have time.

 Where do you feel the pain?

Where is your cap?

 I wish I knew where he was!

 Which credit cards can I use?

Which subject do you like the best?

 The driver told us which bus we should take.

 I am going out for a while.

I fell asleep while reading.

 I was told to wait for a while.

 Who is she?

Who built it?

 Go and see who it is.

 I wonder why.

Why do you ask?

 Nobody knows why.

 I will never tell anyone about this!

Will it rain today?

 This will do for now.

Come with Donald.

I agree with you.

We see with our eyes.

We cannot live without water.

He left without saying goodbye.

He likes coffee without sugar.

 This plan might work.

The engine does not work.

 I have to go to work.

 Ken was in Japan last year.

I will be sick every year.

 Where did you live last year?

Try it out!

Fill in the blanks with the words that are provided in the boxes below.

| with | where | why | work | who | what |

I have to go to _____ .

I know _____ to do.

I agree _____ you.

_____ is your cap?

I wonder _____ !

_____ built it!

Try it out!

Write your own sentence based on the sight words given below.

| with | where | why | work | who | what |

CROSSWORD

Challenge yourself to a crossword puzzle.

Across

1. _____ is your cap?
2. Nobody knows ____.
3. He likes coffee _____ sugar.
4. I fell asleep while reading.

Down

5. Ken was in Japan last _____.
6. I know _____ to do.
7. Which credit cards can I use?
8. Will it rain today?

1. Where 2. Why 3. Without 4. While 5. Year 6. What 7. Which 8. Will

 I am not ready yet.

He hasn't yet come.

 Why didn't you have your lunch yet?

 Thank you!

Are you OK?

 How are you?

 Young people like popmusic.

I wish we were young.

 Peter looks very young.

 It is your book.

Clean your room.

 Put your hat on.

The zebra is related to the horse.

Zebra have beautiful skin.

Zebra runs at 40 mph.

It's zero degrees.

Count from zero to ten.

One comes after zero.

ZIG-ZAG

It's a zig-zag path up the hill.

The male moth flies in a zigzag patern.

The road to home is zigzag.

ZIPPER

She used the zipper on her bag.

How do I fix the zipper on my Jacket?

I broke the zipper.

ZOO

 They work at the zoo.

Does every city have a zoo?

 I went to the zoo yesterday.

ZOOM

 This button is used to zoom.

The camera zoomed on the landscape.

 Zoom into search.

Try it out!

Fill in the blanks with the words that are provided in the boxes below.

| zoo | you | yet | young | zipper | zebra |

I broke the _____.

_____ have a beautiful skin.

How are _____?

They work at the _____.

I am not ready _____.

Peter looks very _____.

Try it out!

Write your own sentence based on the sight words given below.

| zoo | you | yet | young | zipper | zebra |

Challenge yourself to a picture sudoku.

Solution:

Try it out!

Fill in the blanks with the words that are provided in the boxes below.

| want | so | there | right | when | on |

I am _____ happy!

I _____ a guitar.

_____ was in finished?

_____ is no doubt.

Put your hat _____.

That is _____ right!

Try it out!

Write your own sentence based on the sight words given below.

| want | so | there | right | when | on |

CROSSWORD

Challenge yourself to a crossword puzzle.

Across

1. Do you have any _____ questions?
2. Did you say _____?
3. I am _____ tired.
4. There is a cat _____ the tree.
5. The road to home is _____.

Down

6. I _____ she was sick.
7. She goes to _____.
8. Peter looks very _____.

1. Other 2. Something 3. Really 4. Under 5. Zig-Zag 6. Thought 7. School 8. Young

Made in the USA
Las Vegas, NV
15 December 2021